For Kate

First edition for the United States published 1997 Barron's Educational Series, Inc.
Text collection copyright © Macmillan Children's Books 1997
Illustrations copyright © Axel Scheffler 1997

Published by arrangement with Macmillan Children's Books

All inquiries should addressed to:
Barron's Educational Series, Inc.
250 Wireless Boulevard
Hauppauge, New York 11788

International Standard Book No. 0-7641-5056-1

Library of Congress Catalog Card No. 97-8289

Printed in Italy

9 8 7 6 5 4 3 2 1

Let Sleeping Dogs Lie
and Other Proverbs
from
Around the World

Axel Scheffler

BARRON'S

CONTENTS

INTRODUCTION

In England, it's best to let sleeping dogs lie. In Hungary, wise men know better than to make the goat their gardener. When in China, you should try to avoid suspicion by not lacing your shoes in a melon field.

Every country has its proverbs, each one reflecting the wisdom, humor, and way of life of its people. Often the same thoughts are expressed by different cultures in different ways. In North America, for instance, the silent hog eats the most acorns, while in Tanzania it's the silent beetle that eats all the seeds.

Sometimes, however, the meaning behind a proverb can be very elusive. Why, for instance, did the Romans say that an ungrateful man is like a tub full of holes? Why do the Turks remind themselves not to turn up their trousers before they get to the brook? Clearly, many proverbs are open to interpretation and could easily fit into more than one of the categories in this book.

It can be hard to pinpoint a proverb's country of origin. By their very nature, proverbs tend to have been around for hundreds, if not thousands, of years and it's not easy to work out who said them first. Under each proverb, we have indicated which country or culture we believe created it. Sometimes, we've had to admit defeat and leave the country of origin as unknown.

No collection of this kind can hope to be exhaustive. However, we hope that readers will be enriched, enlightened, and entertained by this selective sampling of all the wisdom of the world.

LUCK

If you have escaped the jaws
of the crocodile while bathing
in the river, you will surely
meet a leopard on the way.

West Africa

Running away through
fear of a scorpion,
he falls into
the jaws of
a poisonous
snake.
Sanskrit

If you throw
a handful of stones,
at least one
will hit.
India

While a man is driving a tiger away from
his front door, a wolf is entering the back.

China

When roubles fall from
heaven there is no sack;

when there is a sack
roubles don't fall.

Russia

Throw him into the river and he will rise
with a fish in his mouth.

Arabia

Stay near the tree so
that the fruits may fall on you.

Holland

The tortoise's food is eaten by others.
Without quick legs what can he do?

Zambia

The heaviest
rains fall
on the
leakiest
house.
Japan

If I peddle salt, it rains;
if I peddle flour,
the wind blows.

Japan

WISDOM

A wise man does not make
the goat his gardener.

Hungary

It is foolish to hold a
candle before the sun
or turn somersaults
before a donkey.

India

The hen with
a worm in
its bill will
not cackle.
Unknown

The wise man avoids meeting the angry bull.

Yoruba

Wise is the man
who has two loaves,
and sells one to
buy a lily.

China

If there were wisdom in beards,
all goats would be prophets.

Armenia

A foolish man waters an elephant
with a spoon.

Persia

The old elephant knows where to find water.

South Africa

The giraffe is wise:
he never makes a
noise and he can
see far away.

Tanzania

The tortoise is the wisest.
He carries his own home.

Bambara

A wise man sits on the hole
in his carpet.
Persia

Better to sit with
an owl than to
fly with a falcon.

Germany

OPPORTUNITY

Make hay while
the sun shines.

Spain

Where you hear there are plenty of cherries, always carry a small basket.

Greece

The silent hog eats the most acorns.
North America

The silent beetle eats the seeds.
Tanzania

A sleeping cat
will not catch a rat.
India

The tortoise wins the race while
the hare is sleeping.

Unknown

The early bird
catches the worm.
Unknown

The fox that waited
for the chickens to fall
from their perching place
went hungry.

Greece

ENVY

When everyone praised
the peacock for his
beautiful tail, the birds
cried out with one voice,
"But look at his legs
and what a voice!"

Japan

Your cracked jug seems better to me
than my sound one.

Spain

One potter envies another.

Unknown

Our neighbor's crop seems better
than our own.

Latin

Your neighbor's apples are the sweetest.

Yiddish

He who gives to
others' dogs is
barked at by his own.

Italy

The grass is always greener on the other side of the fence. *Unknown*

The cow from afar gives plenty of milk.

France

INJUSTICE

The smallest boy
always carries
the biggest fiddle.
England

An ox with long horns,
even if he does not butt,
will be accused
of butting.

Malay

The dog stole and the goat is being punished.

West Africa

The worst hog often gets the best pear.

Italy

The cat steals the rice
and the dog comes
and eats it.
China

The sparrow says, "I did not eat, therefore
the parrot should not eat."
West Africa

A fox should not be on the jury
at a goose's trial.

England

PATIENCE

The monkey learns to jump
by trying again and again.

West Africa

Don't bargain for
fish while they
are still in
the water.
China

A hasty man
drinks tea with
his fork.
India

A watched pot never boils.

Unknown

If you run after
two hares,
you will catch neither.

German

The leaping cow finds little food.

West Africa

Go slowly, says the chameleon, and
you'll find something to eat.

West Africa

With one hand
    he feeds the hens,
        with the other
            he searches
               for eggs.

Armenia

Don't count
   your chickens
      before they
        are hatched.

Unknown

He that would have eggs must endure
the cackling of hens.

Greece

Hair by hair, you may pluck out
the whole beard.

Russia

Don't turn up your trousers before
you get to the brook.

Turkey

APPEARANCE

If the baboon could
see his own behind
he would laugh too.

Kenya

It is only when the cold season comes
that we know the pine and cypress
to be evergreens.

China

A chicken with beautiful plumage
does not sit in a corner.

West Africa

He that has a big
nose thinks everyone
speaks of it.

Scotland

The monkey has a big mouth because,
he says, otherwise he would be too pretty.

Ewe

The polecat does not know it stinks.

Zulu

The price of your hat isn't the
measure of your brain.

America

Don't remind
a vain man
of his pimples.

Russia

Dress up a stick and it does not appear
to be a stick.

Spain

A man with a sour face should not
open a shop.

Japan

FRIENDSHIP

In the friendship of the ass,
expect nothing but kicks.

India

A hedge between keeps friendships green.

France

Two sparrows on one ear of corn
make an ill agreement.

Unknown

Monkeys pick fruit together.
Liberia

Birds in their little nests agree.
England

If two men quarrel,
even their dogs
have a difference.
Japan

The cat and dog
may kiss, yet are none
the better friends.
Unknown

If you step
    on one ant,
        the others come
           to bite you too.
               West Africa

EXPERIENCE

To know the road ahead,
ask those coming back.

China

Only when you have crossed the river can you
say the crocodile has a lump on his snout.

Ashanti

He who has been bitten
by a snake fears
a piece of string. *Persia*

He who was bitten by the snake
avoids the tall grass. *China*

Don't sit on the horse's nose no matter
how much you know about horses.

Bambara

Only the wearer knows where the shoe pinches.

England

Only he that has traveled the road knows where the holes are deep.

China

Caution

If you take the wrong hat
from the meeting, make sure
it doesn't belong to a big man.

Ireland

When two hippopotamuses quarrel,
don't put your oar in.

Bugunda

Look before you leap.

England

Let sleeping dogs lie.
England

Do not speak of secrets in a field
that is full of little hills.

Hebrew

When the fox preaches,
keep an eye on your geese.

Germany

The chameleon does not leave one tree
until he is sure of another.

Arabia

Make friends with
the wolf, but keep
your axe ready.

Russia

Do not step
on the tail of
a sleeping dog.

Turkey

Trust in God, but tie your camel.

Persia

IMPOSSIBILITIES

You cannot find a striped
squirrel in every hollow
fence pole.

North America

Two watermelons cannot be held
in one hand.

Persia

You cannot dig a well
with a needle.
England

You cannot send a chicken
to bring home a fox.
Ireland

The cow cannot
jump about the
tree like a squirrel.

Germany

Frowning frogs cannot stop the cows
drinking from the pool.

Kikuyu

You cannot catch lions with cobwebs.
North America

If you walk on snow you cannot
hide your footprints.   *China*

You cannot make
a crab walk straight.
Greek

Without oars you cannot cross in a boat.

Japan

A man alone cannot push a boat into the sea.

Swahili

A cat with gloves cannot catch mice.

Greece

One cannot shoe a running horse.

Holland

You cannot hang everything on one nail.

Russia

There is not enough
room for two feet
in one shoe. *Greece*

GRATITUDE

Do not blame God for having
created the tiger, but thank him
for not having given it wings.

India

Praise the bridge that carried you over.

England

Don't look a gift horse
in the mouth.

Unknown

An ungrateful man is like a tub full of holes.

Latin

Scratch my back
and I'll scratch yours.

Latin

Do not bite the hand
that feeds you.

Unknown

Do not cut down the tree
that gives you shade.

Arabia

CONSEQUENCES

Those who have one foot
in the canoe and one foot
in the boat are going to
fall in the river.
Tuscarora

If you have a monkey under
your blanket, it will move
and make a bulge.
  South Africa

He that blows on the fire will get sparks
  in his eyes.

Germany

He that steals honey should watch out
for the sting.

China

If the camel gets his nose in the tent,
his body will soon follow.

Arabia

When nuts grow ripe, hogs grow fat.
North America

Touch black paint and you will have black fingers.
China

If you bring your firebrand into your hut then do not complain of the smoke.

West Africa

An arrow shot upright falls on the shooter's head.

Unknown

If you sleep with a dog you will rise
full of fleas.

Greece

When one dog barks, the pack joins in.

Germany

AGE

Every age wants its playthings.

France

To succeed, consult
three old people.
China

To an old man the smallest hill
seems like a mountain.
Jewish

It is good
to follow
the old ox.
Unknown

The baby crocodile doesn't cry when it falls
into the water.

West Africa

Old goats love green young leaves.

West Africa

When a wolf walks lame, the old rabbit jumps.

North America

An old broom knows the dirty corners best.

Ireland

CONTENTMENT

A dirty hog in the house
is better than no hog at all.

North America

A sparrow in the bush is better
than a vulture flying.
Blackfoot

A trout in the pot is worth
two salmon in the sea.
Ireland

I have plenty of apples and pears,
but my heart
yearns for
quince.

Armenia

If there is no apple, one eats a little carrot.

Russia

A feather in the hand
is better than a bird
in the tree. *England*

A pullet in the pen is worth a hundred
in the fen. *Unknown*

A bird in the hand
is worth two in the bush.

Greece

When the bed breaks, there is the ground
to lie on.

India

AND FINALLY ...

If you would avoid suspicion,
don't lace your shoes in
a melon field.

China

The squirrel might be small, but he's not
the elephant's slave.   *Unknown*

He that has his hand
   in the lion's mouth
      must take it out
         the best way he can.
Scotland

Since my house is burning, I may as well
      warm myself at it.
Italy

Though the bird may
fly over your head,
let it not make its
nest in your hair.

Denmark

He who has never seen a castle
will admire a pigsty.

Yugoslavia

The frog saw the horse being shod and presented his feet also. *Turkey*

Ten tailors will sew your garment badly.

Do not give ruffles to him who wants a shirt. *England*

Do not dress in leaf-made clothes when going to put out a fire. *China*